AF265470

Bullying Elimination Handbook

The complete guide on how to eliminate and prevent all forms of bullying.

plus additional resources through free download

By

Stuart Macmillan

Copyright©2011 Stuart Macmillan

All rights reserved. No part of this book may be reproduced or used in any form or by any means, electronic or physically, including photocopying, recording, blog, social network or by any information storage or retrieval system or library without obtaining prior permission in writing from the author. Inquiries should be addressed to the address below.

Published by:
Character Education Programmes of New Zealand (CEPNZ)
PO Box 20-616, Glen Eden, Auckland 0641
New Zealand

www.cepnz.com and www.cepnz.co.nz

ISBN: 978-0-9582903-6-4

CONTENTS

DOWNLOADS

Note: Throughout this book you will find smaller images and references to other resources to be used in conjunction with these guidelines. These can be downloaded for **free** from our website using your free membership password. Any item with "(download)" after it can be obtained for free from this link.

To receive your password, send an email to the publisher at info@cepnz.co.nz with your name and address. You will then receive a question by return email asking you for a number of words from specific lines on specific pages to verify that you have purchased this book.

Once you email these words back to the publisher, you will be emailed the website link and your password to access the free material and updates.

INTRODUCTION

Bullying of all forms needs to be eliminated. This book is designed to equip teachers with the skills needed to reduce all forms of bullying and help all schools to implement strategies that reflect a zero-tolerance to bullying.

The resources in this book and through the free downloads will provide your school with guidelines to help eliminate all forms of bullying from within your grounds and within your local community.

Take the examples and guides within this book and use them in talks with your students. Download the additional free material associated with the examples in this book and help make your school a safer and more enjoyable place for the children of your community.

There is *NO* excuse for being a bully!
BULLY
Friendship is stronger than anger.

DEALING WITH PHONE-TEXT BULLYING

Mobile phones and other devices are not the root of the problem; it is the person behind the phone that can be the problem.

The only way that a school can solve the problem of text bullying is NOT by banning the use of the item but by regulating and monitoring its use within your grounds and according to your terms and conditions.

On the previous introduction page you find links to various resources that will be referred to on this page. These items are to be introduced into school policy in order to regulate and monitor the use of mobile phones on your school grounds.

The first step, if it is not already in place, is to ensure that it is made clear that ALL mobile phones are switched OFF during class time. Teachers could introduce a "3 strikes" method in the classroom in order to drive home the message: First a warning to switch the phone off; second, a warning to switch off or it will be confiscated; third, confiscate the phone until the end of the day.

That takes care of interruptions and the possibility of text bullying during class hours.

The next steps will ensure the complete monitoring and regulation of the use of mobile phones within the school grounds.

Regulation:

Use the forms from the free download section to regulate the use of mobile phones within your school.

The first form - **Mobile Record Card for students to complete** (download) should be given or made available to all students.

Record Your Mobile Number:
Name: ....
Class: ....
Mobile Number: ....
Alternate Number: ....

Return this card to the school office and prove your number to staff to obtain a mobile permission card. If you do not record your number to the office, your mobile phone may be confiscated.

It must be made clear that unless a student completes one of these forms to register the number of their mobile phone and hands it into the office, their phone will be confiscated for the rest of the school term.

At least a weeks grace should be given to do this and parents should be notified of your school policy regarding the regulation of the use of mobile phones within the school through your newsletter. This way, when your policy is enforced and a mobile phone is not registered, both the parents and the students will be fully aware of the consequences.

At the same time display posters (download) throughout your school. These posters remind students that the number of their mobile phones must be registered with your school office

When the student completes the form and returns it to the office (or their teacher, a staff will verify that the number they have listed on the form is the same as the phone they are carrying by asking them to show the phone number on the screen of their phone.

Once the verification is complete, the student is given a permission slip to carry the phone on school grounds (download). This form should also be stamped with the school stamp to avoid duplication by students.

Permission to carry a Mobile Phone
This card entitles the named person to carry the listed mobile phone on school grounds if displaying the school stamp.

Name: ....

Mobile Number: ....

This card and the number on your mobile phone must be shown on demand to any staff member, prefect or designated monitor upon request.

The student should also be cautioned that this form should be carried on them at all times while at school and must be presented upon request or the phone may be confiscated.

All mobile phone numbers should be recorded on a database for future reference. A copy of an Excel sheet made for this purpose can be downloaded. As you will see from the example, we suggest that all teachers have their mobile phone numbers recorded by the office as well for safety sake. It may never happen but if a student reports abuse of texting, it would be a good idea to be able to clear school staff as well.

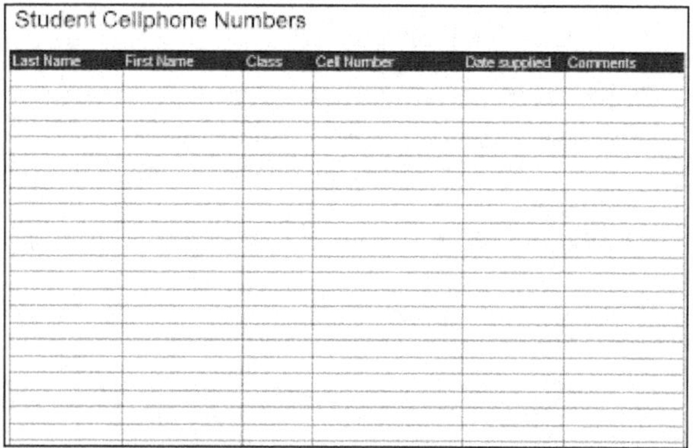

Reporting:

Text abuse report cards (download). These should be copied and made readily available from teachers or the office or handed out to every student.

> I have received a nasty text or email
> The phone number was:
>
> ....
> Or, the email address was:
>
> ....
> The message read:
>
> ....
> ....
> ....
> (Hand this form into the school office)

If a student then receives a threatening or abusive text on their mobile phone or by email, the details can then be recorded on this form and handed to their teacher or the office. The form advises the student to keep a copy of the abusive text showing the phone number as proof when they report the abuse. This should be viewed by the staff member to whom it is reported for verification and witnessing.

Compare the mobile number listed in their report to your database of mobile phones and you will have the method of locating the offender when the database is completed.

Bully Tips:
1. Do not feel bad about being bullied; it is the bully that has the problem, NOT you.
2. If you are being bullied in ANY way, report it immediately.
3. If you get a nasty text or email, do NOT reply to it but keep a copy of it and report it immediately.
4. People who ask for help are strong, be strong and ask. Others DO care!

Always ensure that parents are aware of your procedures and ask them for a list of all mobile phones their children own. This can be done through a newsletter or asked at a parent-teacher evening. Remember to state that this is a safety precaution to enable their child to be eliminated from any future investigations or reports of textual abuse.

Actions:

Textual and email abuse is an offence. There are a number of posters contained in your free downloads that display this fact and these should be printed and displayed around your school. Some are worded harsher than others but they do help to drive the message home!

Your school probably already has a set of procedures for dealing with abuse or bullying within your grounds. Here are some tips to ensure that all bases are covered:

- Ensure that all communications are kept confidential between staff, parents and the students involved.
- Advise the parents concerned as soon as possible (both of the offender and the victim).
- Make an appointment for the parents to visit the school to discuss the matter and outline the options of possible resolutions to the offence.
- If the offence is continuous, follow your procedures to involve the Police in further discussions.
- If the bullying is by mobile phone, ban the offender from carrying it on school grounds.
- Refer the offender to your Anti-Bullying Student Council, Tribunal or mediation (see the section below on this).

Whatever your standard procedures are, ensure these are carried out swiftly and that the victim is assured that your school will support her or him at all times. They need to know that you do care about their welfare at all times.

It would also be a good idea to make the "I Need Help" cards available at different locations around the school (download). These are designed so that students that have a problem but don't know who to ask will be able to fill it in and hand it to their teacher or staff member.

CYBER-BULLYING

STUDENT GUIDELINES ON HOW TO DEAL WITH AND SAFELY REPORT CYBER-BULLYING

The Internet is a great way to find information from all over the world. As more and more people are finding it easier to get connected these days, there are also a lot of bad and sick-minded people out there who get pleasure from hurting others.

If you are using chat-rooms or places such as Bebo, Facebook or MySpace, the chances are that at some time you will come across one of these people. Therefore you should always be prepared and do not trust the words of strangers or anyone that you are not absolutely "*sure*" about.

So, what is cyber-bullying?

Cyber-Bullying can take many forms. The simplest form of cyber-bullying happens in Emails. These can be sent by someone you know or from someone who has found your email address online or has been given it by someone else. If you have an email address, only give to those people that you know you can trust and ask them never to give it to anyone else without your permission. If you have been given the email address of a friend from that actual person, treat them with respect and never give it to anyone else.

If you receive an email from someone you know that contains hurtful words or offensive content, ask them politely to stop. If they do not stop sending this type of email immediately, tell your Mum or Dad or another adult you can trust such as your teacher. Never reply to nasty emails by sending nasty emails back to them. Make sure you keep a copy of all these emails right from the beginning as these will be needed as evidence. Remember, you are the victim and it is *NOT* your fault!

Some of the worst offenders of Email bullying may even tell you to do something for them or send money to them in order for their offending to stop. These types of emails should be reported to the Police immediately!

Another form of bullying can take place in Blogs. Blogs are places on the Internet where people can record a journal or their opinions on the News or events happening around the world. Some people use blogs in the wrong way by writing nasty words about other people they know and even display pictures of people caught in embarrassing situations. This is another form of bullying and if you know of any website that is listing mean or nasty words about you or anyone else you know, write down the Internet address of that website and give it to your Mum or Dad or your teacher. These websites should be reported to the Police immediately (don't phone 111 but have an adult phone the local Police station as they have teams of officers that know how to deal with this sort of thing.

The same type of offensive material can also appear on personal Bebo pages, discussion forums, chat rooms or through Skype or similar voice over the Internet systems (called Voip). They should all be reported and dealt with in the same manner.

A known example of this is where a teenage girl joined a chat room looking for a friend. A male started up a nice conversation with her and over time she thought he was her perfect match and gave out her phone number so they could chat more (NEVER DO THIS!) and her address so they could write to each other (NEVER, *NEVER* DO THIS EITHER!).

The situation ended up with more than three different men ringing her saying they were from the KGB and they knew where she lived and where her new Internet boy friend lived and would hurt her, the boy or a member of her family if she told anyone else and unless she started sending money to a Post Office Box in Tauranga.

The girl did not tell her Mother about it or report it to the Police because she believed her "boy friend" (the *false* identity she met in the chat room) would be hurt. Instead she started sending money she had saved up from her after-school and holiday job to the address she was told to. She was cleaned out of $8,000 before it as brought to an end!

The way this could all have been stopped would have been if the girl had told her Mum about it in the first place and had it reported to the Police. Also, as stated before, she should *never* have given her name, phone number or address to a stranger!

As in this case, it is the person receiving the threats that is the victim. It is NOT your fault if this happens so REPORT IT IMMEDIATELY! If you are involved with online chatting, keep a record and always talk about it with a member of your family so they can guide you in the right direction. Always use a false name and a free email address that can't be traced. Better still, if you want to meet someone, avoid the Internet chat rooms and be more sociable with your friends and people that you already know and can trust.

These types of threats are serious and should be dealt with as soon as they start! If you have experienced any sort of bullying or threats on the Internet, do NOT try to "laugh it away" or just ignore it. Report it immediately and you could also be helping the other person before they get into deep trouble with the Police.

BUT ... do NOT try to "help" the other person your self if you are the victim or reply to them in any way.

STUDENT GUIDELINES ON DEALING WITH BULLYING

Provide your students with these guides

Assurance:

Ensure that your students know that it is your schools obligation and determination to *"provide a safe physical and emotional environment"*.

Not only that but the staff of your school are fully committed to this responsibility and will play an active part to ensure that any student that becomes the victim of abuse, in what ever form, will be listened to and supported.

Further more, your school is fully committed to ensure that the offence of bullying will not be tolerated in any form and every measure will be taken under the law to bring any offender to justice.

Measures:

Bully Tips:
1. Do not feel bad about being bullied; it is the bully that has the problem, NOT you.
2. If you are being bullied in ANY way, report it immediately.
3. If you get a nasty text or email, do NOT reply to it but keep a copy of it and report it immediately.
4. People who ask for help are strong, be strong and ask. Others DO care!

Give every student a copy of the support card – they are in your free downloads.

It is best that these guidelines are mentioned and expanded upon at least once every two weeks at your school assembly. For this, you may want to use some or all of the comments that are listed below.

What Students should do:

You should use these pointers to expand upon your discussion on the guidelines for students on how to correctly deal with bullying and to avoid and report any occurrences.

Bullying:

(Also see the chapter, "Eliminating Gang-Mentality")

A bully is just another person the same as you and I. The only difference is that the bully feels that they need to act in a certain way towards others that is hurtful in order for them to feel good.

The main ingredient to *feeling* good is actually *being* good and acting nice yourself. In this manner you can attract other people to be your friends simply because they want to be around your good natured company.

The only problem is that when you act good, play nicely and are generally good natured toward others, you can also attract the attention of the opposite type of people...the bully.

The reason for this is that the bully is seeing something around or about you that they want...happiness and friendship. The only way the bully thinks that she or he can gain what you have is to try and take it away from you and impress others that think the same way as they do. This way, they feel that *they* are getting the attention and respect they deeply desire.

We all know that the way in which the bully goes about attention seeking is wrong. In actual fact, the actions of the bully are a criminal offence! This is why this type of action can no longer be tolerated in our schools or our communities.

If you are being bullied or see someone else being bullied, it is your responsibility as a caring member of our society to report it at once!

You may think to yourself that this is 'snitching' or telling tales or that you may face a worse reaction from the bully but the opposite is true. Unless you are prepared to make a stand against bullying, it will continue or get worse...make sure you report it.

As for your actions toward the bully, there are a number of steps you should take:

- Do NOT confront the bully in the same manner in which she or he is acting.

- If at all possible, ignore the actions or the words of the bully and remove yourself quietly from the area in which the bullying is taking place to a more crowded or friendlier area.

- If the bullying is being carried out by email or mobile phone texting, do NOT reply to the messages but keep them as proof of the action when you report it to your teacher, staff member or parent.

- If you are being called names, don't worry about it. Names won't get you into trouble but the actions of the bully could eventually land them in jail in later life.

- If the actions of the bully are making you feel sad, follow the directions below headed "Happy Exercises".

- REPORT IT!

At all costs, avoid the bully. Don't be drawn into arguments with them, just report their actions to your teacher or a staff member or use one of the forms provided to seek help.

Happy Exercises:

If you are feeling sad or your feelings have been hurt, here are a few things that are guaranteed to make you feel better.

Think about this for a moment: "How do I get sad?" What you are asking here is not what *things* make you feel sad but how do you actually *become* sad?

Did you know that it is what you say to yourself, how you think and how you stand, walk and talk that make you feel sad?

Here's an exercise - next time you are feeling sad, think about *what* you are thinking about. You are probably thinking about the *things* that you don't like that are making you sad. How are you standing or sitting? Are you slouched in a chair or are you standing with your chin on your chest and your shoulders slumped forward? How are you breathing? Is your breath very shallow, hardly noticeable?

All of these things are making you *feel* sad. Now do this...

Stand or sit up straight. Pull your shoulders back. Lift your head up as if you are trying to see over someone in front of you and take a few deep breaths. Think about what you want to get out of life when you get older...the success, the good grades, the great job, the car, the house, the happiness and put a smile on your face and when you talk, talk as if the person if you are talking to is at the other end of the room (but don't shout).

If you were crying before, you won't be now! If you were sad before, you will feel more confident now! See, it works! It is a proven scientific fact that *you* are in total control of your emotions and the way you think simply by acting, standing, talking and thinking in a manner that is entirely different to the way you currently feel.

Always remember that you are in charge of your own mind and your own emotions. Your success or failure totally depend on your outlook on life and what you tell yourself. But remember, ALL troubles can be halved if you tell someone else about it. NEVER let *yourself* stand in your own way forward to happiness and ALWAYS ask for help if you need it.

Stuart Macmillan

ELIMINATING GANG-MENTALITY

It has been said that the reason why a person acts as a bully is either because the bully has been bullied themselves at sometime in the past or that they are bullied or abused by a family member. Another excuse for being a bully could be the lower income level of the family that they are a part of and their inability to reach goals that require money.

All of these are just excuses! The reason why people become bullies or part of a gang is because they do not think highly enough of themselves. These types of people are attracted to other people of the same disposition as themselves. They all have low self worth.

Let's take an example: There are a pair of twin brothers that live at home with a Father that drinks a lot and takes drugs. There is never enough money in the house and always a lot of abuse. Twenty years later, one of the twins has grown up to be like his Father, the other to be a Doctor.

What was the difference? The one that grew up to be like his Father thought that if it was all right for his Dad to be like that with a roof over his head and booze in his hand all day, then it's cool enough for him too!

The son that grew up to be a Doctor thought that there was no way that he wanted to live a life like that so he set his goals above his present surroundings to find a way out and live a better and happier life and that by becoming a Doctor, he might be able to help his brother and his Dad.

Life doesn't always end up like stories do but the fact of the matter is that every person is in control of their own destiny, whether to success, failure or crime.

With this in mind, how does a school help to eliminate gang mentality?

The correct education of the child is the first and best way to curb the development of this type of association. I hear you say that this is not the job of the teacher! You are quite correct. This is the job of the parents!

The problem is, there are a growing number of parents in our communities that either simply don't care about the moral up-bringing of their children or they just don't have any morals of their own in the first place. It is not where the blame lies that we should be looking at but trying to find a solution to the problem.

What we have to say is, "what are we going to do about it?"

The best thing that your school can do to address this problem is to take its own course of action in the realms of education and your responsibility to provide a safe physical and emotional environment within your school.

Let us have a look at a few ways in which this can be done:

- Ban the wearing of all gang related regalia within your school grounds. This includes ear-rings, bandannas, arm patches, etc.

- Pick some extracts from the guidelines below and put these into class discussions or assembly addresses.

- Get students and teachers involved with developing "Classroom Declarations" (see the later chapter) towards a school-wide, student-initiated charter that will set standards of behaviour within the class and school.

Guidelines for Students:

Peer pressure is probably one of the heaviest burdens outside of your school work that you will face in your young life.

Part of that pressure is going to involve influence from others to try and get you to do something that may be against your nature in order to feel welcomed into a group or gang. This is the type of peer pressure that you need to avoid.

The only group that you should feel that you want to be a part of are those that have the same respect for life as you do...your friends in other words. Friends are NOT people that expect you to act like a sheep and follow along with what others do. Nor will they expect you to do something, dress in a certain way or act in a particular way around them or toward others.

If you are feeling pressure from those around you to do something that is against your first instincts, don't do it! If this is the case, you obviously need to find some new friends.

What you need to do is to find out what it is that you want to achieve within your own life. You need to set yourself some goals and discover what you will need to do in order to reach those goals. If one of those goals is to succeed in life and pass your exams, it becomes obvious that there are things that you should be doing and other things that you should be avoiding.

Let's say that one of your immediate goals is to get a good end of term report card or a pass in next months test. In order to do that, you are going to have to make sure that you do all the work, homework and assignments that your teachers set for you. If on the other hand you are receiving pressure from friends, or groups that SAY they are your friends, to go out with them or to hang around the shops after school (or worse!), these are things that you will need to avoid in order to be able to reach your goals.

Remember the words of Yoda in Star Wars: "Once you start down the dark path, there is no turning back!" This may sound extreme but it does point out that you need to concentrate on your priorities in order to reach your goals. If you follow the advice of these so-called friends, you could loose sight of your goals and perhaps miss the target for the rest of your life.

You WILL find greater satisfaction in reaching one goal after another than you will in becoming *accepted* by a group that may not have any goals at all apart from getting into trouble in the long run!

In order to avoid this negative pressure, all you have to do is state firmly but in a friendly manner, "No thanks, I have other plans." If they were your good friends in the first place, they would respect your wishes and will pressure you no more. If they are the type of people that would eventually get you into trouble, they would be persistent but you need to stand your ground and spend less time with them until they leave you alone.

If the pressure turns into bullying in any form, report it! You didn't need them as friends in the first place.

Further reading for students:

Never be content to just "go with the flow" and follow what others are doing. Sheep follow the leader but leaders make their own decisions and control their own lives. By your good example, others will soon follow your lead and you will be able to help them grow for the better.

You may have heard that you can get happy with alcohol, drugs, sex or fast cars but this is very wrong! People that indulge in such activities for pleasure are only looking for an immediate enjoyment without considering the consequences of their actions. What happiness is there in a hangover? What happiness is there in being sick, not being able to think properly, failing your school work, wasting your money, catching a sexually transmitted disease, getting pregnant at an early age or even dying or killing someone else?

These are the outlets and behaviours of losers! They don't have a chance to reach their long-term goals and aspirations unless they move away from such habits. They don't have a chance to reach full happiness in life unless they remove these abuses from their lives.

You must always keep your focus on your long-term goals that will bring you happiness and fulfilment and avoid failure by keeping in mind the long-term ill-affect and consequences of improper or damaging behaviour.

"What will my friends think?" you may say. If they are true friends, they would appreciate the difference and the changes you are making in your life. If not, you were mixing with the wrong crowd. You have all your life ahead of you to make new friends and believe me you will make many more when you transform your life.

SETTING UP A STUDENT/TEACHER 'BULLY MEDIATION/COURT' SYSTEM

Please note, the steps outlined in this document are guidelines *only*. This system should not be used to ridicule a person and counselling should be sought for stubbourn offenders.

The first steps in setting up a sort of "tribunal" or mediation system to solve resolutions and deal with bullies is to develop a "Student Charter" (see the next chapter).

Option One:

Once you have established the ground rules of the type of behaviour that will not be tolerated in the classroom or within your school, you have a standard on which to set up judgements.

The idea of a tribunal is to have a student council on which will also sit one or two overseeing teachers. This council should be made up of about five respected members of your student body and will be responsible for hearing complaints or resolving conflicts or differences of opinion resulting from the breaking of the Student Charter mentioned in the above document.

Some students that are bullies will not always listen to what their teachers have to say and will go straight back out and do it again. If on the other hand, they know that part of their punishment will be to stand before a council of their own peers to explain their actions, they may think twice about doing it again!

These 'tribunal' (for lack of a better term) hearings can be held once a week in a separate classroom.

These hearings should be carried out as if it were a court session and both parties should be allowed to address the Council as to their position, with the offender allowed to try to defend their actions with just cause and a teacher may speak for either party. Questions should be asked of both parties by the Council in regard to the incident in relation to the rules outlined in their Student Charter.

On the completion of the hearing, the Council should adjourn to discuss the outcome of the hearing and then return to advise the offender that they have been found "Guilty of Bullying" and that these actions will not be tolerated by any student within the school.

A copy of the School Charter should be produced from which the relevant rule that has been broken should be read out for all to hear (preferably by the offender). The offender should then be asked if she/he can see that she/he has broken this rule and is prepared to abide by it in future. The offender should then be free to return to their deans office to discuss the proceedings.

Option Two:

In the same manner as above, a Council is formed from the student body. These students are then designated as seniors to whom students can turn to in order to report a bully if a teacher is not present at the time. The matter is then taken up by the Council member with a teacher who will then take action.

Upon proof of the bullying incident, the Council of students meet in a private room or classroom with the overseeing teachers and the offender. In this meeting the incident is discussed in a quiet manner and the peers of the student are involved with talking to the offender about why this is occurring and the reasons why it is not acceptable within your school.

Please note again, it is not my suggestion to see 'kangaroo' style courts being set up in every school. These are just guidelines to give you ideas on how the peers of the offenders can be involved in assisting with a resolution to the problem.

DEVELOPING "CLASSROOM DECLARATIONS"

In order to fully involve your students in the process of zero tolerance toward bullying, they need to be involved in setting the rules in the first place. The best way to do this is to get them involved in the creation of a "Student Charter" for your school.

The first step in the development of a "Student Charter" for your school is to hold class meetings in which the students and teachers can discuss class and subject goals, rules of conduct and methods of problem and dispute resolution within each classroom. This can then be put together as a mini-charter for the class and a poster can be made up for displaying these 'rules of conduct' where it is easy to view at all times in the classroom. Have each of the students sign this mini-charter and they will feel a part of it and respect it as if it were a type of "Constitution" or "Classroom Declaration" to be upheld.

A copy of each "Classroom Declaration" should be given to the Principal and extracts from each can be combined into the main points (or declarations) of the schools overall "Student Charter".

The Principal should then visit each classroom at an appropriate time and put his/her signature to each of the original "Classroom Declarations". This action alone will show her/his commitment and connection to each of the students within the school if it is carried out with honest respect and admiration for the work accomplished by the students.

This same practice should be carried out for the type of behaviour that is to be expected and the types of behaviour that will not be tolerated in the playground and on the sports field. These notices should be clearly displayed in the gymnasium, school hall and inside the doors of exits from school buildings.

If you are a Primary School, use the same guidelines to set up class rules. Get all the kids involved in talking about what is good behaviour and what is bad behaviour. If they are the ones that come up with it, they will then fully understand what is expected of them both in the class and in the playground.

DEALING WITH MISBEHAVIOUR AND THREATS

Unless your school sets specific boundaries for what is expected from your students and what behaviour is considered unacceptable, you will not have the ability to control and deal with problem students.

The best way to do this is to involve all your students and staff in the creation of these boundaries and how to deal with students that cross those lines.

These boundaries can be set forth in a Charter developed using the guidelines set out in the preceding chapter, "Classroom Declaration". In this manner, each of your students will FULLY understand the type of behaviour that will not to tolerated and the consequences that will follow on the breach of these rules.

Suggested steps to follow:

- Try to remain as calm as possible.

- Do not try and sympathise with the student as this can be taken as being patronising instead of displaying real care for the individual.

- Ask the student about what they are trying to accomplish through their actions and the reason why the student is displaying such actions or using such language.

- Suggest an alternative as a means of release or solution to what they are seeking.

- If you are feeling threatened by a student in your class, back away and either place a desk between yourself and the offender or leave the room if this is not an option and call for assistance.

- Report the incident as soon as possible.

Having said that, ALL threats and acts of violence MUST be reported to the parent and the Police without hesitation.

EFFECTIVE TEACHING AND HARNESSING STUDENT ATTENTION

Methods by which your school can engage students and increase their desire to learn include:

1. Ensuring students are fully aware of what is expected from them and why they need to learn specific topics (relate to specific areas in life in which they will benefit from the knowledge gained).

2. Use everyday examples from the local, historical or international community to enhance the subject being taught.

3. In each class, emphasise the importance of developing problem-solving skill that will be effective in life (in general) not just in the classroom.

4. Students should be taught how to set goals, plan their work and study tasks, monitor and manage the work that they are doing and self-evaluate how their work is being done so that they can see the results and how each lesson is fitting together.

5. Give students more control over their own work through self-evaluation and planning (as discussed in previous point) and only intervene when the student is displaying difficulty.

6. Make full use of other learning techniques such as mind mapping, using accompanying music or visual aids to enhance the student's ability to learn and make the learning experience more interesting.

7. Encourage the active participation of the students in the lessons wherever possible,

especially those that are 'slower' learners or mischief-makers.

8. Always discuss any 'problem situation' in terms of virtue and in relation to the Classroom Declaration.

9. Always start a new subject or area of study with a general outline of what it is about and the general principles that are being discussed or that will apply to the subject area.

10. Encourage students to look at a new area of study by first examining techniques or subject areas that they have already learned to see if existing techniques or principles can be used to solve a new type of problem. This way you are showing them how to use existing resources to accomplish new tasks.

11. Look for ways to provide students with opportunities to practice cooperation, teamwork, and responsibility in class projects.

12. Look into developing a breakfast or lunchtime 'club' during which a volunteer teacher and/or senior students can get together with other students that are finding certain areas of study difficult and

create a 'mentor programme'. If some students are showing great talent in subject areas, learning and planning skills, ensure that these talents are put to good use to develop their sense of public service to help other students.

ENHANCING COMMUNICATION SKILLS

The first rule of communication is to always listen. The worst situation you can find yourself in is when you reply to someone before you have actually listened to what they have said and you are sure of what they are saying to you.

The second rule of communication is to be certain that the words you are using will accurately convey the message you are trying to put across.

Misunderstandings in communication occur when the message is not put across in the right manner.

When you are the communicator you must ensure that the words that you use, the tone of your voice and your facial expressions as well will accurately represent the message you are putting across.

Well chosen words can have a great effect on the class you are instructing, in conflict resolution and in general conversation. You must keep in mind that not everyone has the same meaning in their head to some words that you may use.

you really mean but what will the other person think of in their mind? You could be meaning something like "the sun was like a glowing orange ball with yellow steaks coming from it", or you could be talking about the use of swear words.

Make your choice of words represent the actual idea you are trying to convey and never be vague or your words may be lost in translation. Ensure the same rule is followed when typing written assignment, reports and letters and always read your own work - don't rely on the spell checker on your processor (see the light hearted look at this on the next page).

Also, in order to communicate your lessons to your students, you need to use your voice and facial expressions to show your passion for the subject you are teaching. If you are not interested in what you are talking about, do you really think that your class will be?

Effective communication of ideas in the classroom will need to include a bit of humour. A little light-heartedness on the subject goes down well.

Vary the tone, volume and pitch of your voice to stress certain points. This can also be used to catch your class off-guard and make them pay more attention or wake them up by putting less stress where they may expect there to be more stress and visa-versa.

INVOLVING PARENTS AND YOUR COMMUNITY

Looking for early signs of anti-social behaviour and how to best deal with it before it develops and what to do if it occurs.

We all know that parents are your students primary care givers and providers. It is their responsibility to bring up their children properly, not the schools. Part of this responsibility includes being the moral educators of their children to such an extent that the child is well aware of what type of behaviour is acceptable and what is *not* acceptable in society.

The problem is that a number of parents are not being the type of role-models that their children need to develop good character and pro-social behavioural principles. This being the case, schools and teachers are being put in the position of trying to cope with anti-social and disruptive behaviour in their students that should have been straightened out by their parents at an early age.

Schools do not exist to be social workers for their community but they do play a big part in helping to shape young minds through the environment of the school as a microcosm of society. It is in the school that the child first experiences the wider world and has to mix with people that come from different backgrounds, cultures and even languages.

For this reason, the school needs to fully involve parents and the local community to help with this transition into the wider world and any behavioural difficulties and problems that may manifest in the child at school.

Recognising and Dealing with Disruptive Behaviour:

Any early signs that a child is tending toward any form of disruptive behaviour in school must be immediately reported to the parents. Before this happens, the school should always ask the parents if the child has any special needs of disabilities at the time of enrolment and during any subsequent parent interviews.

Early signs of disruptive behaviour can include:

- Talking to others in class when they should be listening to the teacher.

- Talking too much and interrupting others during a classroom discussion.

- Changing the subject when talked to.

- Writing and passing notes to other students.

- Arriving too early or late at school.

- Eating or drinking in class.

- Looking out the window or around the room - not paying attention.

- Negative interaction with other children - name calling, pulling faces, taking others' property, general bullying.

If any of these symptoms become apparent, the parents should be notified at the earliest time. Questions should once again be asked as to whether the child has any eyesight or hearing problems which can effect the behaviour of the child. It can also be suggested that the child is tested for glue-ear as this problem can cause a child to become increasingly disruptive.

Reason:

In a survey of 200 inmates of Mt.Eden Prison in Auckland, New Zealand:

- All 100 Maori (Polynesian) prisoners checked had hearing loss ten times worse than the national average.

- Eighty-two percent of non-Maori prisoners had the same degree of hearing loss.

- Most of it stemmed from lack of hearing checks and treatment in early childhood.

Source: Pacific Network Magazine (February 1992).

From these statistics, could some of these people have been prevented from becoming criminals if their parents had checked their hearing at an early stage? This message should be driven home to ALL parents.

If the particular behaviour continues to cause problems, organise a meeting for the parent to come in to the school to discuss the behaviour that is causing a disturbance. Make sure that this is done in front of the student so that the problem can be discussed openly to try to discover any underlying reason for the behaviour to exist.

Involving Parents in School Processes and Policies

All parents should be made aware of your schools policy on zero tolerance to behaviour that can cause harm to others or interferes with day to day life at school.

Organise and advertise an open day assembly for parents. This can be held after school or on a weekend or school holiday. The purpose of this assembly will be to make it known that your school is dedicated to providing a safe and secure environment for all students and staff.

At this assembly it should be stressed that your school will use all legal resources at its disposal to eliminate bullying, intimidation and all forms of anti-social behaviour. Any actions that deemed harmful or threatening to any member of the staff, student body or the community will be dealt with.

Make it known that your school expects every parent to fulfill their parental responsibility in ensuring that they know what their children are up to and actively encourage their children in the arts of pro-social behaviour.

At the same time, ensure that the parents know that they are always welcome to make an appointment to discuss the performance of their children and any issues relating to their behaviour or worries they may have in relation to the behaviour of other students toward their own children.

At the assembly, make available a form for parent to pick up on entering or leaving on which they may make any suggestions on school policy with regard handling behavioural problems of students in the community. These forms should be returned to the school within one week (while the discussion is still fresh in their mind) and should be discussed at your next Board of Trustees or PTA meeting.

BULLYING IN THE WORKPLACE

Bullying in the workplace can take many forms. These forms of bullying can be from co-workers or from students or parents. The types of bullying can include:

- Emotional

- Physical

- Sexual

- More than one of the above

All of these types of bullying (as is the same case with students against each other) are forms of *abuse*. They can not be tolerated in any form or at any time.

These categories of abuse can take shape as the calling of names, non-official threats against employment or salary, physical violence (even if it is stepping on someone's toe), sexual harassment by staff or pupils or even neglect through isolation from access to resources or assistance.

Whatever form it takes, if you as a teacher are the brunt of any form of abuse or bullying, it must be reported.

DISCOVERING THE TRUTH IN YOUR STUDENTS

In order to be able to discover if your students are telling the truth when you ask them questions, you will need to discover what their learning style is. Let's take a look at a way in which you can find out how they process the information in order to make your first discovery of their learning style.

Have you ever heard that expression "they eyes are the windows to the soul"? There may be some truth in this as you can find out how a person processes information by watching their eye movements. These eye movements can also tell you what their best learning style is. Let's take a look...

Basically, learning happens through each of the five senses, these can be further reduced to three main categories:

1. Visual (learning by watching, reading and seeing)

2. Auditory (learning through listening and hearing)

3. Kinesthetic (learning by physically doing things - "hands-on" approach)

Just by looking at people's eyes when you ask them questions or talk to them, you can get an instant appraisal of their learning style and how they are processing information in their brain. The examples on the next page are for regular right handed people.

Visual Learning Style

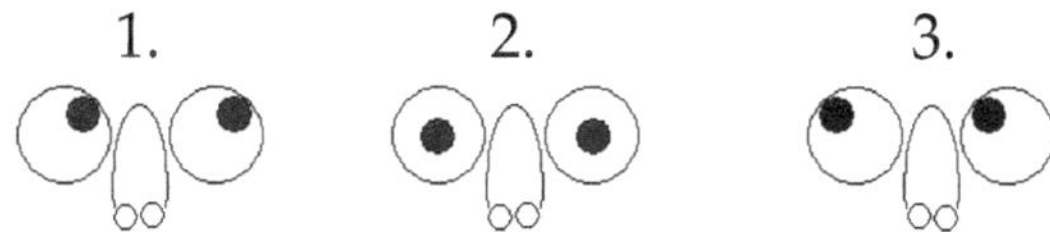

Auditory Learning Style

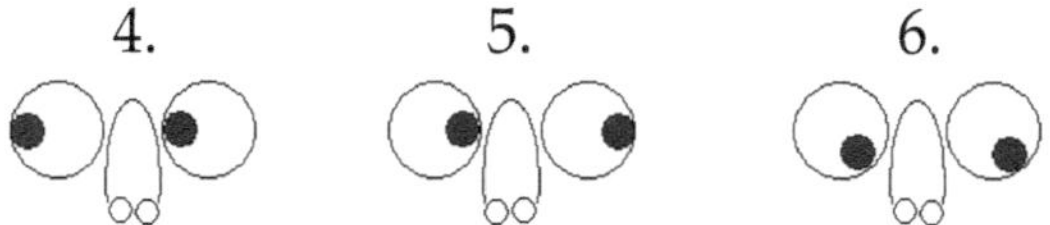

Kinesthetic Learning Style

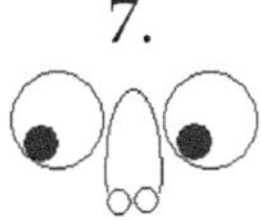

Have you ever noticed that when you ask a question of someone or even enquire about how a persons holiday was, more often than not, they will move their eyes around in one direction or another. This shows you how the person is recalling the information they are talking about.

If they move their eyes upward and to the left or right or look straight ahead as if looking into the distance, they are trying to visualise the answer to the question or remember a picture they have in their head.

If they move their eyes straight toward the left or right or look down and to the left, they are trying to remember what they heard that relates to the question or remember a sound they have in their head (often the voice of the person that gave them the answer in the first place).

If the person looks down and to the right they are recalling actually doing something. It could be writing or building something or the physical sensations associated (temperature, comfort, taste, pain or pleasure) with what is being recalled.

Remember, you need to know if the person is left or right handed first in order for this to be successful.

Try this out now. Remember the position of the eyes when you talk to others and you can turn a mundane conversation into something more challenging and rewarding.

Discovering the Truth:

People who master these techniques of discovering a persons thinking processes can also find out if the person is telling the truth or lying! Imagine the progress you could make in conflict resolution.

Let's take it a little further:

In image 3 the person is looking up and to the right. Although associated with visual recall, the person is trying to visually construct something they have not seen before. Whereas in image 1 the person in recalling something them have actually seen.

In image 4 the person is to the right. Although associated with auditory recall, the person is trying to construct a sound or phrase that they have not heard before. Whereas in image 5 the person in recalling something them have actually heard and in image 6, they are talking to themselves.

In Kinesthetic processing, image 7, the person is trying to recall feelings.

So, from this you will not only be able to find out how your students learn but also how truthful a person is actually being with you. For example, the answer to the simple question "Did you watch the news last night for your assignment?" could be analysed by watching the eye movement. If the person looks up and/or to the right, they are constructing an answer based on imagination. In other words...no they didn't watch the news (if they are right handed remember!).

OTHER TITLES BY
STUART MACMILLAN

Stuart Macmillan

TEACHERS COACH

(co-authored with Elizabeth Macmillan)

Providing teachers with a refreshing look at teaching skills and guidelines to fundamental qualities to enrich the teaching and administration processes.

Available in paperback and ebook through our website:

www.cepnz.co.nz/coach.html

Stuart Macmillan

DYNAMIC LEARNING STYLES

Designed to help anyone from the age of 8 to 80 years old to find out the best way in which they can learn more quickly and effectively and remember what they learn. No long-winded descriptions and unnecessary reading - this book gets straight to the point and teaches the methods quickly and easily from page one. Ideal for teachers, parents, children and adults of all ages.

Available as a E-Book from:

http://tinyurl.com/486dovm

Soon also to be available in paperback

Stuart Macmillan

LITERACY & NUMERACY PACK

The Literacy & Numeracy Pack has all your basic Mathematics and English needs in one place. Not only will this provide you with all you need to know to get on in general life but you will also learn methods to remember things, get on with others better, apply for a job and how to easily perform calculations in your head. Great for the everyday needs of adults and students of all ages.

Available as a E-Book from:

http://tinyurl.com/4ulqljj

Stuart Macmillan

BEING ARDENT ABOUT LIFE

Being Ardent about Life teaches you how to implement the ARDENT personal development programme into your life. You will be shown how to take a closer look at your life, develop and understand your values system, set goals, succeed and enjoy life to its fullest.

"The essential guide to enthusiastically living a passionate, successful, happy and fulfilling life!"

"Change your life for the better in time that it takes to read this book!"

Available in paperback and ebook through our website:

www.beingardent.com

Character Education Programmes of New Zealand
(CEPNZ)
For further insights see our website at:

www.cepnz.com

For the full CD version see:
www.cepnz.co.nz/bully.html
Twitter: twitter.com/cepnz
Blog: http://cepnz.blogspot.com/
Facebook: http://tinyurl.com/25way2a

www.ingramcontent.com/pod-product-compliance
Lightning Source LLC
Chambersburg PA
CBHW061040050726
47592CB00004B/1523